Sub Urbane

Sub Urbane

Poems by

Jason Fisk

© 2021 Jason Fisk. All rights reserved.
This material may not be reproduced in any form, published,
reprinted, recorded, performed, broadcast,
rewritten or redistributed without
the explicit permission of Jason Fisk.
All such actions are strictly prohibited by law.

Cover design by Shay Culligan

ISBN: 978-1-952326-99-8

Kelsay Books
502 South 1040 East, A-119
American Fork, Utah, 84003

To Laura, Delia, Jonas, and Ezra with love

Acknowledgments

Eunoia Review: "Lazy Afternoon," "The Money Artist," "The Giant Exhale," "It's Natural"
Red Eft Review: "Icarus' Daughter," "The Poet's Daughter," "Something Greater," "The AC Went Out," "The Robin's Nest"
Déraciné Magazine: "The Knife Block," "A Christmas Poem in Four Parts"
One Art Poetry: "Across the Street"
Boston Literary Magazine: "Needed Rain," "The Morning After"
The Birds We Piled Loosely: "Summer Memories," "Getaway"
Alternating Current Press: "Exoskeletons"
Wine Cellar Press: "The Scar on My Hand"
Trouville Review: "Paradigm Shift"
Ephemeral Elegies: "Putting the Dog Down"

Contents

Lazy Afternoon	11
Icarus' Daughter	12
The Knife Block	13
A Christmas Poem in Four Parts	14
Across the Street	18
Needed Rain	20
Summer Memories	22
Exoskeletons	23
Getaway	24
The Scar on My Hand	27
The Morning After	28
The Poet's Daughter	29
Something Greater	30
It's Natural	31
Putting the Dog Down	32
Paradigm Shift	33
Hypochondriac	34
The Bird	35
The Money Artist	36
The AC Went Out . . .	38
The Robin's Nest	39
The Giant Exhale	41

Lazy Afternoon

In the suburbs where biblical names
and their derivatives flourish
and for sport we read lost-pet signs
and speculate as to the animal's demise
(My favorite is coyotes)
and we judge the owner's loneliness
by the size of their reward

I sit out back and watch my son
blow bubbles on the tree-shaded deck
I find myself rooting for the bubbles
as they escape on the warm summer breeze
I know that once they clear the roof
their potential is limitless

Icarus' Daughter

She swung
on the rusty
backyard
swing set
pointing her feet
toward the sun
swinging closer
and closer

And then
the chains melted
and the child
fell to the ground
Her tears turned
to steam
halfway
down
her cheeks

A pang of guilt
as her father
watched
from the air-conditioned
comfort of inside
He waved
when she looked
to see if he saw

The Knife Block

Part I
The dense wood-block knife holder
we got for our wedding sits solidly
on our countertop and we pretend
that all the knives are there and
that they're just somewhere
in the household wash cycle
but that's not true—they're not
Some have disappeared over time
and if I start thinking about everything
that's disappeared over time
I become paralyzed with sadness
thinking about the blackhole
that exists at the center of time
carving away hunks of life

Part II
I read you the poem
about the wood-block
knife holder
and you said you
hated it and asked
if that's how I felt
about our marriage
and I said *No*
because I love you
and adore being
married to you
but I also asked
*Can't I just write
a sad poem about
a knife holder?*

A Christmas Poem in Four Parts

Part I
Winter holidays were
just around the corner
and five of us went
out after work
We were sitting
around the fireplace
in leather chairs
drinking wine and beer
and our conversation
splintered from the three
others and you talked about
a poem I had written
and how the vulnerability
was just too much
and how others
called it beautiful
but you just couldn't
bring yourself to call it that
and then I told you about
how I hated the holidays
because Christmases were awful
and I rambled on about one
where we couldn't open
presents for an hour after
we woke up because our parents
were arguing in their bedroom

and then the one where a church
bought our family presents
because we were poor
and I was like, *What? We're poor?*

and the moment we got
off our bus to start Christmas break
and mom sat us down and told us
that she had packed our things
and that we were leaving dad
and we spent a month living in a motel

and the Christmas where my sister
was with me at college in Chicago
and she was suicidal
and I got her out of the hospital
and I spent evenings with her at the hotel
during her outpatient treatment
and how one evening we were watching
It's a Wonderful Life
and I started crying at the end
and I looked over, and she was asleep
The new meds made her tired
and I felt alone

You nodded
and I stopped talking
and looked around
at the silence
and the other three
had been listening
so I stopped talking
because I tend
to share way too much

Part II
At a holiday party he told me
that he had heard or read
that people who overshare

either grew up poor
or were not very intelligent
and that thought hung on me
like the smoke from the fireplace
In the car on the way home
I was suffocated by the thought's smell
Was I stupid?
I had to roll down the window
And absorb the cold air

Part III
I enjoy the Christmas tree
the most the week between
Christmas and New Year's Eve

That week
it is free of
weighted
expectations
social gatherings
and anxiety

Part IV
I write about Christmas
to fill the blackhole
inside with something
other than emptiness
and replayed
worn-out
conversations

And when I'm done
for a moment
I feel relief
My sky no longer
sags and threatens
to fall like a heavy
curtain on a final act

In that moment
I see moon wisps
that smell like
cotton candy vapors
and I taste eternity
and it soothes my dry
cracked brain

When I write
my head expels
everything in it
like a shark turning
its stomach inside out
purging
what it can't digest

And I start over
on another line
Unease
wrung
from me
like water from
a sponge

Across the Street

We live in the suburbs
and we have a Ring Doorbell
and we have a tiny dog
and there are coyotes
that live in the woods
across the street

I let the dog out
every night before bed
and watch her sniff
the air for dangerous news
blowing from
our coyote neighbors
across the street

I keep an aluminum baseball bat
by the front door
just in case the coyotes
decide to attack her
or try to lure her
back across the street

My imagination has
 played out a scenario
where they surround her
and I come thundering
out of the house swinging
the bat left and right
taking out one coyote after another
knocking them here and there
sending them yelping back
to the woods
across the street

I think about the rush
I would get from
posting the Ring-Doorbell video
on Facebook

Every *like* a micro dose
of adrenaline

Needed Rain

The storm will be here by nine he said
so we should be at the bar before that
We can get a few drinks
sit in the upstairs patio
and watch it roll in
One long island and three beers later
the rain fell big
and the sky blazed blue

Then, a text from my wife
Wife: stay as long as you need to I know about his mom
Me: ?
Wife: she has cancer
Wife: brain
Wife: please don't say anything
Wife: unless he does. his wife told me earlier this evening.
Wife: it's bad
Me: he's said nothing…
Wife: sorry. he won't even talk to his wife.
Me: he's just carrying on…
Wife: he probably just needs to get out

On the way home
I opened the windows and sunroof
and drops of old rain landed on our heads
we laughed
He reached over and cranked the radio
Dylan sang
there must be some way out of here
said the joker to the thief
there's too much confusion here
I can't get no relief

His driveway
He shook my hand
got out of the car
and walked into
his dark house

Summer Memories

My daughter's black
rubber bottomed flip-flops
haphazardly kicked off beside
my son's canvas Keens
lying on the splinter prone parquet
floor in the middle of the yellow walled hall
My sundried beer-soaked brain
thought it was something beautiful
something worth noting
The size of their small feet
The forgivable stink of childhood

Exoskeletons

Sitting on my neighbor's new patio furniture
shaded from the summer sun by the huge umbrella
drinking beer and watching her daughter
smash small vacuous cicada shells
on the concrete
with an oversized red plastic bat

I hated that he spent
all of his time out here my neighbor said
but now I understand
I've spent a lot of time out here this summer
drinking and thinking she said
staring at her beer
as it were the first time
she'd seen it

How's she handling it? I asked
pointing the neck of my beer
toward her daughter

Fine . . . I think . . .
I just hope I don't make her a man hater...
I'm constantly having to keep myself in check
Like right now . . .
I want to tell her to smash the hell
outta those empty cicada shells
That's what men become
after you live with them
for six-and-a-half years
just empty shells . . .
better gone than here . . .
But I hold my tongue
and let her enjoy
her simple destruction . . .

Getaway

I looked out the hotel room window
The TV flickered in the dark room
and the kid's slept
Their wind-burnt faces
poked out from beneath better
bedding than we had at home

I poured red wine into the thick hotel glass
and felt the ease of alcohol unwind
the city anxiety from my shoulders
as the gritty red stained my teeth

I looked at Lake Michigan
eleven floors below
It was not yet frozen
I was removed
from the sound
removed
from the people

The city lights made dirty
yellow glow circles on the beach
and I watched joggers' tiny breath
rhythmically expelled
from their bitty bodies as they passed
through the yellow light glow

And then I saw him
He walked briskly
toward the water's edge
and didn't stop
He walked straight
into the water
fully clothed

Holy shit, I whispered
What? my wife asked
and walked over
just in time
to see him go under
and not come up
. . . still underwater
still not coming up

We should call someone,
she whispered

Let them sleep, I said
I pulled the blinds
and quickly finished
my glass of wine
*I'll go down and call
from the front desk*

I sat at the hotel bar
and ordered another
glass of wine
and as I sipped
I drifted further
and further
from the urgency
of the moment
and with each
passing second

I became less sure
of how to explain
what I'd just seen
to anyone
especially
the people
at the front desk

The Scar on My Hand

My wife and I sat in the car after grocery shopping,
and I reached for the hand sanitizer.
What's that? she asked, pointing to a scar on my hand.
Oh, that's from my sister, I said,
touching the forty-year-old scar.

Instantly, I flashed back to
when I was eight, and our family
had been given an assorted meat and cheese gift basket.
My sister had been cutting the cheese and sausages
with the miniature meat cleaver that came with the set,
and we started to argue about who got what,
and, like happened so often back then, we got into a fight.
I went to hit her, and she instinctively
raised the miniature meat cleaver.
The blade was about two-and-a-half-inches long.
I ended up punching the cleaver and not my sister.

She laughed
and I bled.

She is gone now.
I miss her.

I'm glad I have the memory.

The Morning After

I walked out for the newspaper
and heard the birds chirping
Their crisp twittering songs
circling strong in the still air
And for the first time in my life
I realized that mornings magnify sound

I went to get the mail after the storm
and the fresh-earth scent
was the most enthralling
aroma I had ever inhaled
And for the first time in my life
I realized that rain magnifies smell

And later that night
after a few hours of sleep
I woke up
alone
and I felt a deep sorrow
like never before
And I realized that
silence
magnifies mistakes

The Poet's Daughter

She sat in the theater's dimness
and watched a movie
with her friends

She suspected a sad ending
so she pulled out her phone
and looked it up

She just had to know

Warm tears traced tributaries
down her cheeks
as she read the spoiler
in the chilly theater

She wiped her eyes
slid the phone into her pocket
and watched it all unfurl
on the massive screen before her

And despite already knowing
How it would end
she cried as
the credits
rolled

Something Greater

The sun embraces the evening
Its shadows angle across the burb
Rain clings to the sidewalk's pores
The storm is still troubling the air
Red wine and teriyaki salmon
fill my belly and on the way home
I crank the music of my youth
Magically, I am sixteen again—invincible
Car soaring down the highway
between two truck trailers
on my way home from school
Wanting to smash into them
just to hear the crinkle of
the car metal
Just to be humbled
by the blunt impact
of something greater than me

But now I have kids
in bed at home
and wonder
how I got
from wanting
to smash my car
to being their father

Something greater
than me

It's Natural

I used to think it was silly
that my dog would always
bring me her toy
and show it to me
always so proud of herself
It seemed so primal, so base
I changed my mind today
when I returned from Costco
and started pulling items from the bag
showing my wife what I'd bought

Putting the Dog Down

My wife said she would make the call if I took the dog in.
My wife had to leave the room to make the call.
She came back: *Go now. They're waiting for you.*

I drove with the dog on my lap.
I paid.
I waited.
There was an adjustable metal table in the room.
I wanted the vet to talk me out of it.
He didn't.
He gave me a few minutes.
A nurse came in and administered two shots.
The dog fell asleep.
The vet came back in—*Blah, blah, blah,* he said.
He gave me time with the dead dog.
I didn't want to sit with the lifeless body.
When he left, I left too.
I looked straight ahead and bolted through the door.
I started to drive home.

I hoped they cradled her body when they moved her, I thought
That metal table was so cold.
Winnie . . . my little dog . . . gone.

I was overcome.
I couldn't see through my tears well enough to drive.
I pulled over.
I cried for twenty minutes in the industrial park.
I ignored my wife's texts.
I ignored her phone calls.

Her phone calls . . .

Paradigm Shift

The sun waltzed across
the planks of the deck
peeking from between
the dancing leaf shadows
and I steadied my four-year-old
as he stood barefoot on the railing
and we watched the robin
feed her three fledglings
dropping earth-colored worms
into their begging beaks

Where do the babies go poop and pee? he asked

I guess they go in the nest, I said

That's gross, he said.

It is, I said, having never
thought about it before

Now
somehow
watching the birds
in their nest
is different

Hypochondriac

I piled the boys into the car
and drove to the doctor's office
and the doctor eventually saw us
and examined my son
who had strep throat
He wrote a prescription
So we drove to the pharmacy
and my son cried
while sitting in the red plastic chair
because he couldn't get comfortable
because he couldn't swallow
and an old woman stared at me
like I didn't know my son was crying
on the red plastic chair
And we waited in line forever
and I sat the baby's car seat
on Walgreen's floor
and rocked him with my foot
I looked around and
saw a diabetic wall display
I saw sugar-free candy
and foot lotion
for diabetics with dry feet
and I thought *I have dry feet,
I wonder if I have diabetes?*
And I looked it up on my phone
while rocking the baby with my foot
and the symptoms didn't quite match
but I bought the lotion anyway
because my foot
suddenly
started
itching

The Bird

It was unavoidable
The bird flew too close
to the car
A natural born Icarus
with wings and feathers
Cursed with the illusion
of immortality

The hobbled bird
bounced
hopping
side to side
Upright on one leg
then falling to its side
confused—stunned

I drove by the next day
looking for
nothing
wanting to see
nothing
and I saw its carcass
against the curb
claws clutching at
nothing

And I wondered if foisting
too much meaning
on everyday occurrences
was my curse

Would I be happier
if I saw nothing
but a dead bird?

The Money Artist

He loved how the paper submitted to his will
folding under the pressure of his fingers
Each crease held feeling
Every paper pleat possessed love

He hated the unappreciative
after he gave his folded paper away
Their indifference heightened his insecurities
Unfortunately, some people were immune to his art
to his skill
to his creations

He did find that people took him more seriously
when they saw the care he put into his craft
the love he put into his dyed paper dragons
so he opened a street-side studio
where he displayed himself
in the window
making paper hydras
and he priced them
according to his labor—his love

And he failed
and his shop cost him money
and his wife was not happy
Then he had an idea—
He took paper money
from his bank
from his past
for his future
and folded the dollars
into mini green monsters
The coarseness of the currency
calloused his fingers

and his heart grew weary
but he made money

Not a lot
Just enough
to keep
him
going

The AC Went Out . . .

. . . and I laid on the basement floor
trying to get below the heat
I was binge-watching a TV show
because that's what one does
when it's too hot to move
As the night rolled around
and my binge program moved
into its fifth season
and I couldn't sleep
because it was too hot
and the air was too thick
I heard flies and bugs hurling
themselves against the window screen
trying to get inside
the house for some reason
Maybe it was the glow
of the television
that attracted them
As I sat there, I thought
about how they were hurling
themselves against the screen
with everything they could muster
but I had to listen hard
to even hear the flick of their bodies
against the screen
and I thought about how that's a lot like life
but that's as far as the thought went
It's just way too hot to think beyond that

The Robin's Nest

—for Jim Harrison

The nest was mud wedged
into the crotch of the tree
and for weeks my family
watched the process
standing on tippy toes
peering from the edge
of our deck

We watched as beaks opened
to receive food from mama bird
and we saw them grow
crowded in the nest
and they stood on the edge

flapping

their

wings

testing their new equipment

And then one morning
I came out with my coffee
and the nest that had once
been the center
of so much activity
and attention
was now empty

I thought about going over
to the base of the tree
to make sure that they all
made it out, but I didn't
have the heart especially
after reading that half
of new birds don't live
through their first year

Up to one billion birds die every year
Where do all the bird bodies go?
Do they just disappear to heaven?
Are they really angels?

The Giant Exhale

The winter exposes the bones of the landscape,
the skeleton of the world.
I have cried at the table because the meal
brought me back to who I used to be.
It was easier to put a dog down when I was younger;
now, my proximity to death scares me.
I took pictures at her funeral to prove
to HR that these were actually bereavement days.
My mind blurred as I read his poems.
I wanted the words to bend one way
and they didn't. I wished he was drunk.
Listening to Tupac's "Brenda Had a Baby"
and I cried at the lines, "She didn't know
what to throw away and what to keep."
How the fuck did he know that?
That's fucking sad and brilliant.
And while I was meditating,
I forgot to breathe in.
I exhaled my life out through my nose.
I will be so happy when the currency
of the flesh is no longer at war
with my internal life,
but that might be the GIANT exhale.
The loss of that tension might
equal the loss of drive.
Letting it all go.
Letting it all out.
Forgetting to breathe
                        in.

About the Author

Jason Fisk lives and writes in the suburbs of Chicago. He has worked in a psychiatric unit, labored in a cabinet factory, and mixed cement for a bricklayer. He was born in Ohio, raised in Minnesota, and has spent the last twenty-five years in the Chicago area.

www.jasonfisk.com

Kelsay Books

www.ingramcontent.com/pod-product-compliance
Lightning Source LLC
Chambersburg PA
CBHW071641090426
42738CB00013B/3178